This book belongs to

_____

With special thanks to the following people
for their help with translations:

Sylvia Pellarolo, *C.Phil. in Hispanic Languages, U.C.L.A.*
Dominique Abensour, *C.Phil in French and English Languages, U.C.L.A.*
Wolfgang Doering, *C.Phil. in Germanic Languages, U.C.L.A.*

A Rooster Book/September 1994

"Rooster Books" and the portrayal of a rooster are trademarks of
Bantam Doubleday Dell Publishing Group, Inc.

Manufactured in the U.S.A.

Rooster Books are published by Bantam Doubleday Dell Books for Young Readers,
a division of Bantam Doubleday Dell Publishing Group, Inc., 1540 Broadway, New York, NY 10036.

My Home

Illustrations by Lisa-Theresa Lenthall

ROOSTER BOOKS

BANTAM DOUBLEDAY DELL
NEW YORK • TORONTO • LONDON • SYDNEY • AUCKLAND

window   (**WIHN**-doh)

la ventana   (lah vehn-**TAH**-nah)

la fenêtre   (lah fuh-**NEH**-truh)

das Fenster   (dus **FEN**-stuh)

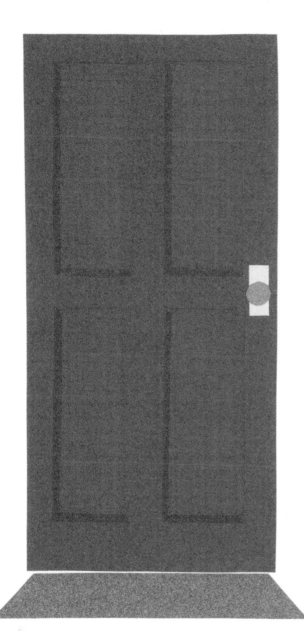

door (**DOR**)

la puerta (lah **PWEHR**-tah)

la porte (lah **PORT**)

die Tür (dee **TEWR**)

table (**TAY**-buhl)

la mesa (lah **MEH**-sah)

la table (lah **TAH**-bluh)

der Tisch (dehr **TIHSH**)

chair (**CHAYR**)

la silla (lah **SEE**-yah)

la chaise (lah **SHEHZ**)

der Stuhl (dehr **SHTOOL**)

lamp (**LAAMP**)

la lámpara (lah **LAHM**-pah-rah)

la lampe (lah **LAHMP**)

die Lampe (dee **LUM**-puh)

sofa (**SOH**-fuh)

el sofá (ehl soh-**FAH**)

le canapé (luh **KA**-na-pay)

das Sofa (dus **SOH**-fah)

sink **(SIHNK)**

el fregadero (ehl freh-gah-**DEH**-roh)

le lavabo (luh **LAH**-vah-boh)

das Waschbecken (dus **VAHSH**-behk-ehn)

towel (**TOW**-uhl)

la toalla (lah toh-**AH**-yah)

l'essuie-main (leh-**SWEE**-maa)

das Handtuch (dus **HUN**-toogh)

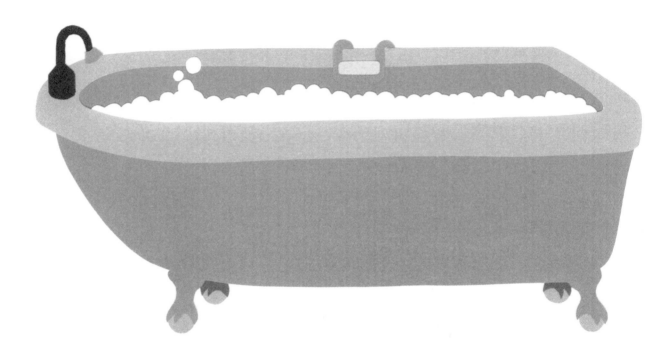

bathtub (**BAATH**-tuhb)

la bañera (lah bahn-**YEH**-rah)

le bain (luh **BAN**)

die Badewanne (dee **BAH**-deh-vun-nuh)

toilet (**TOY**-luht)

el retrete (ehl reh-**TREH**-teh)

la toilette (lah **TWAH**-leht)

die Toilette (dee toy-**LET**-tuh)

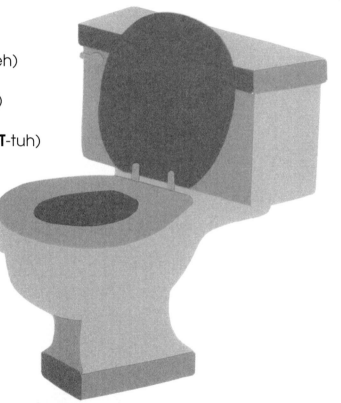

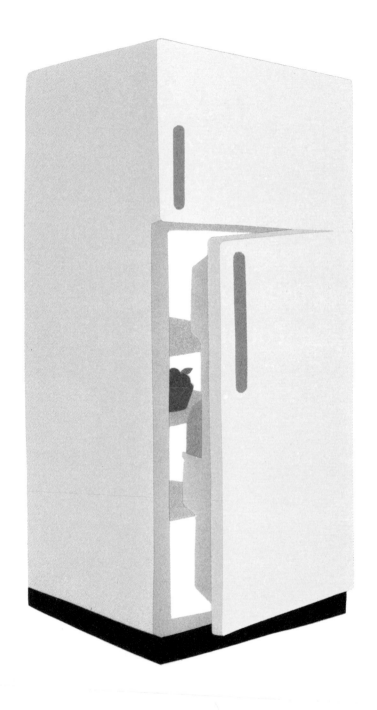

refrigerator
(ree-**FRIHJ**-uh-ray-ter)

el refrigerador
(ehl reh-free-heh-rah-**DOR**)

le réfrigérateur
(luh ray-free-zhay-**RAH**-ter)

der Kühlschrank
(dehr **KEWL**-shrunk)

stove (**STOHV**)

la estufa (lah ehs-**TOO**-fah)

le fourneau (luh **FOOHR**-noh)

der Kochherd (dehr **KOGH**-hehrt)

telephone **(TEH**-luh-fohn)

el teléfono (ehl teh-**LEH**-foh-noh)

le téléphone (luh tay-**LAY**-fohn)

das Telefon (dus **TEH**-leh-fohn)

television   (**TEH**-luh-vihzh-uhn)

la televisión   (lah teh-leh-vee-**SEEON**)

la télévision   (lah tay-lay-**VEE**-zhon)

der Fernseher   (dehr **FEHRN**-zeh-ehr)

bed (**BEHD**)

la cama (lah **KAH**-mah)

le lit (luh **LEE**)

das Bett (dus **BEHT**)

pillow (**PIHL**-loh)

la almohada (lah ahl-moh-**AH**-dah)

l'oreiller (loh-**RAY**-yay)

das Kopfkissen (dus **KOPF**-kis-suhn)

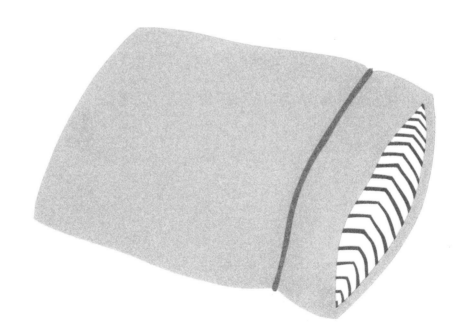